Festive Christmas Cookies

Gingerbread People

½ cup (1 stick) butter, softened
½ cup packed brown sugar
⅓ cup water
⅓ cup molasses
1 egg
4 cups all-purpose flour
2 teaspoons baking soda
1 teaspoon ground ginger
½ teaspoon ground allspice
½ teaspoon ground cinnamon
½ teaspoon ground cloves
    White or colored frostings

1. Beat butter and brown sugar in large bowl with electric mixer at medium speed until creamy. Add water, molasses and egg; beat until well blended. Add flour, baking soda, ginger, allspice, cinnamon and cloves; beat until well blended. Wrap dough tightly with plastic wrap; refrigerate about 2 hours or until firm.

2. Preheat oven to 350°F. Grease cookie sheets. Roll out dough on lightly floured surface with lightly floured rolling pin to ⅛-inch thickness. Cut with cookie cutter. Place cutouts 2 inches apart on prepared cookie sheets.

3. Bake 12 to 15 minutes or until set. Cool 1 minute on cookie sheets. Remove to wire racks to cool completely. Decorate with frostings as desired. Store in airtight containers.

Makes about 4½ dozen cookies

Chocolate Pistachio Cookies

2 cups shelled pistachio nuts, finely chopped, divided
1¾ cups all-purpose flour
¼ cup unsweetened cocoa powder
¾ teaspoon baking soda
½ teaspoon salt
¾ cup plus 1 tablespoon I CAN'T BELIEVE IT'S NOT BUTTER!®
   Spread, divided
1 cup granulated sugar
¾ cup firmly packed brown sugar
2 eggs
3 squares (1 ounce each) unsweetened chocolate, melted
½ teaspoon vanilla extract
⅛ teaspoon almond extract
1½ squares (1 ounce each) unsweetened chocolate
2 tablespoons confectioners' sugar

Preheat oven to 375°F. Spray baking sheets with I Can't Believe It's Not Butter!® Spray; set aside. Reserve 3 tablespoons nuts.

In medium bowl, mix flour, cocoa, baking soda and salt. In large bowl, beat ¾ cup I Can't Believe It's Not Butter!® Spread and sugars until fluffy, about 5 minutes. Add eggs, one at a time, beating 30 seconds after each addition. Beat in melted chocolate and extracts. Beat in flour mixture just until blended. Stir in nuts.

On prepared baking sheets, drop dough by rounded tablespoonfuls, 1 inch apart. Bake one sheet at a time 8 minutes or until tops are puffed and dry but still soft when touched. *Do not overbake.* On wire rack, cool 5 minutes; remove from sheets and cool completely.

For icing, in microwave-safe bowl, melt 1½ squares chocolate with remaining 1 tablespoon I Can't Believe It's Not Butter! Spread at HIGH (Full Power) 1 minute; stir until smooth. Stir in confectioners' sugar. Spread ¼ teaspoon icing on each cookie; top with reserved nuts. Let stand 20 minutes.   *Makes about 3½ dozen cookies*

Chocolate Pistachio Cookies

Eggnog Cookies

Cookies

    1 cup (2 sticks) unsalted butter, softened

  1¼ cups plus 1 tablespoon granulated sugar, divided

    1 egg yolk

    ½ cup sour cream

  2½ cups all-purpose flour

    ¼ teaspoon salt

    ½ teaspoon grated nutmeg

    ¼ teaspoon ground ginger

Filling

    ½ cup (1 stick) unsalted butter, at room temperature

    ¼ cup shortening

  2½ cups powdered sugar

    2 tablespoons brandy or milk

1. Preheat oven to 350°F. Lightly grease cookie sheets.

2. For cookies, beat butter and 1¼ cups granulated sugar in large bowl with electric mixer at medium speed until light and fluffy. Add egg yolk; beat until blended. Add sour cream; beat until well blended. Combine flour and salt in small bowl. Gradually add flour mixture to butter mixture, beating until well blended.

3. Shape rounded teaspoonfuls dough into balls. Place on prepared cookie sheets; flatten slightly. Combine remaining 1 tablespoon granulated sugar, nutmeg and ginger in small bowl; sprinkle over cookies.

4. Bake about 12 minutes or until edges are golden. Cool 5 minutes on cookie sheets. Remove to wire racks to cool completely.

5. For filling, beat butter and shortening in medium bowl until well blended. Add powdered sugar and brandy; beat until well blended. Spread or pipe filling on bottoms of half the cooled cookies. Top with remaining cookies.   *Makes about 6 dozen cookies*

Ginger Shortbread Delight

Cookies

> 1 cup (2 sticks) unsalted butter, softened
> ½ cup powdered sugar
> ⅓ cup packed light brown sugar
> ½ teaspoon salt
> 2 cups minus 2 tablespoons all-purpose flour
> 4 ounces crystallized ginger

Glaze

> 1 bar (3 to 3.5 ounces) bittersweet chocolate, chopped
> 2 tablespoons unsalted butter
> 2 tablespoons heavy cream
> 1 tablespoon powdered sugar
> ⅛ teaspoon salt

1. Preheat oven to 300°F.

2. For cookies, beat butter, sugars and salt in large bowl with electric mixer at medium speed until creamy. Gradually add flour, beating until well blended.

3. Shape tablespoonfuls dough into balls. Place 1 inch apart on ungreased cookie sheets; flatten to ½-inch thickness. Cut ginger into ¼-inch-thick slices. Place 1 slice ginger on top of each cookie.*

4. Bake 20 minutes or until set and lightly browned. Cool 5 minutes on cookie sheets. Remove to wire racks to cool completely.

5. For glaze, melt chocolate and butter in top of double boiler over hot, not boiling, water. Remove from heat. Add cream, powdered sugar and salt; stir until smooth.

6. Drizzle glaze over cookies. Let stand about 30 minutes or until glaze is set.   *Makes about 3½ dozen cookies*

*If crystallized ginger is unavailable, place pecan or walnut half in center of each cookie before baking.

Two-Toned Biscotti with Pistachios and Chocolate Raisins

⅔ cup granulated sugar
⅓ cup butter, softened
2 teaspoons baking powder
⅛ teaspoon salt
2 eggs
2 cups all-purpose flour
¼ cup chopped pistachio nuts
2 tablespoons unsweetened cocoa powder
½ cup chocolate-covered raisins
¼ teaspoon ground nutmeg

1. Preheat oven to 375°F. Lightly grease 2 large cookie sheets.

2. Beat sugar and butter in large bowl with electric mixer at medium speed until light and fluffy. Add baking powder and salt; beat until well blended. Add eggs, one at a time, beating well after each addition. Gradually add flour, beating until well blended.

3. Divide dough in half. Stir nuts and cocoa into 1 portion of dough. Stir raisins and nutmeg into remaining dough. Divide each dough mixture in half.

4. Pat 1 portion chocolate dough into 8×6-inch rectangle. Shape 1 portion raisin dough into log; place in center of rectangle. Wrap chocolate dough around log, flattening slightly; place on prepared cookie sheet, seam side down. Repeat with remaining dough.

5. Bake 40 to 50 minutes or until logs sound slightly hollow when tapped. Cool on cookie sheets 15 to 20 minutes or until warm but not hot. *Reduce oven temperature to 325°F.*

6. Cut warm logs diagonally into ¾-inch slices with sharp serrated knife. Place cut side down on ungreased cookie sheets. Bake 7 to 8 minutes. Turn slices over; bake 7 to 8 minutes or until crisp.
Makes about 2 dozen cookies

Two-Toned Biscotti with Pistachios and Chocolate Raisins

Gingersnaps

2½ cups all-purpose flour
1½ teaspoons ground ginger
1 teaspoon baking soda
1 teaspoon ground allspice
½ teaspoon salt
1½ cups sugar
2 tablespoons margarine, softened
½ cup MOTT'S® Apple Sauce
¼ cup GRANDMA'S® Molasses

1. Preheat oven to 375°F. Spray cookie sheet with nonstick cooking spray.

2. In medium bowl, sift together flour, ginger, baking soda, allspice and salt.

3. In large bowl, beat sugar and margarine with electric mixer at medium speed until blended. Whisk in apple sauce and molasses.

4. Add flour mixture to apple sauce mixture; stir until well blended.

5. Drop rounded tablespoonfuls of dough 1 inch apart onto prepared cookie sheet. Flatten each slightly with moistened fingertips.

6. Bake 12 to 15 minutes or until firm. Cool completely on wire rack.   *Makes 3 dozen cookies*

Mint Chocolate Delights

Cookies
- ½ cup (1 stick) unsalted butter, softened
- ½ cup granulated sugar
- ⅓ cup packed light brown sugar
- ⅓ cup semisweet chocolate chips, melted
- 1 egg, beaten
- ½ teaspoon vanilla
- 1½ cups all-purpose flour
- ¼ cup unsweetened cocoa powder
- ¼ teaspoon salt

Filling
- 2½ cups powdered sugar
- ½ cup (1 stick) unsalted butter, softened
- ¼ teaspoon salt
- ½ teaspoon mint extract
- 3 to 4 drops red food coloring
- 2 to 3 tablespoons milk or half-and-half

1. For cookies, beat butter and sugars in bowl until creamy. Add melted chocolate, egg and vanilla; beat until blended, scraping down bowl occasionally. Mix flour, cocoa and salt in bowl. Gradually add flour mixture, beating until well blended. Shape dough into 16-inch log. Wrap in plastic wrap; refrigerate 1 hour or until firm.

2. Preheat oven to 400°F. Grease cookie sheets and line with parchment paper. Cut log into ⅓-inch slices; place on prepared cookie sheets. Bake 10 to 12 minutes or until set. Cool 5 minutes on cookie sheets. Remove to wire racks to cool completely.

3. For filling, beat powdered sugar, butter and salt in bowl until blended. Add mint extract and food coloring; beat until evenly tinted. Add enough milk, 1 tablespoon at a time, to make filling fluffy. Spread or pipe filling on bottoms of half the cooled cookies. Top with remaining cookies. *Makes 24 sandwich cookies*

Browned Butter Spritz Cookies

1½ cups (3 sticks) unsalted butter
½ cup granulated sugar
¼ cup powdered sugar
1 egg yolk
1 teaspoon vanilla
⅛ teaspoon almond extract
2½ cups all-purpose flour
¼ cup cake flour
¼ teaspoon salt

1. Heat butter in heavy medium saucepan over medium heat until melted and light amber in color, stirring often; transfer to bowl. Cover; refrigerate 2 hours or until solid. Let butter stand at room temperature about 15 minutes to soften before completing recipe.

2. Preheat oven to 350°F. Beat browned butter, granulated sugar and powdered sugar in large bowl with electric mixer at medium speed until light and fluffy. Add egg yolk, vanilla and almond extract; beat until well blended.

3. Combine all-purpose flour, cake flour and salt in small bowl. Add flour mixture to butter mixture; beat until well blended.

4. Fit cookie press with desired plate (or change plates for different shapes after first batch). Fill press with dough; press dough 1 inch apart onto ungreased cookie sheets. Bake 10 to 12 minutes or until just lightly browned. Cool 5 minutes on cookie sheets; transfer to wire racks to cool completely.   *Makes about 8 dozen cookies*

Tip: To add holiday sparkle to these delicious cookies, before baking, sprinkle them with red or green decorating sugar, or press red or green glacé cherry halves into the cookie centers. For pretty trees or wreaths, tint the dough with green food coloring before using the tree or wreath plate in your cookie press. Sprinkle with colored nonpareils for ornaments before baking, or pipe red icing bows on the baked and cooled cookies.

Cinnamon Nut Chocolate Spirals

1½ cups all-purpose flour
¼ teaspoon salt
¾ cup sugar, divided
⅓ cup plus 3 tablespoons butter, softened and divided
1 egg
1 cup mini semisweet chocolate chips
1 cup very finely chopped walnuts
2 teaspoons ground cinnamon

1. Combine flour and salt in small bowl; set aside. Beat ½ cup sugar and ⅓ cup butter in large bowl with electric mixer at medium speed until light and fluffy. Add egg; beat until blended. Gradually add flour mixture, beating until well blended. Dough will be stiff. (If necessary, knead dough by hand until it holds together.)

2. Roll out dough between 2 sheets of waxed paper into 12×10-inch rectangle. Remove waxed paper from top of rectangle.

3. Combine chocolate chips, walnuts, remaining ¼ cup sugar and cinnamon in medium bowl. Melt remaining 3 tablespoons butter; stir into chocolate chip mixture. (Chips will partially melt.) Spread mixture evenly over dough leaving ½-inch border on long edges.

4. Using bottom sheet of waxed paper as guide and starting at long side, tightly roll up dough jelly-roll style, removing waxed paper as you roll. Wrap in plastic wrap; refrigerate 30 minutes to 1 hour.

5. Preheat oven to 350°F. Lightly grease cookie sheets. Unwrap dough. Cut log into ½-inch slices. Place slices 2 inches apart on prepared cookie sheets.

6. Bake 14 minutes or until edges are light golden brown. Remove to wire racks to cool completely.   *Makes about 2 dozen cookies*

Mocha Madness

Cookies

   ½ cup (1 stick) unsalted butter, softened

   ½ cup packed light brown sugar

   ¼ cup granulated sugar

   1 egg

   1 teaspoon vanilla

   1 cup all-purpose flour

   ½ teaspoon *each* salt and baking soda

   ½ cup chopped pecans

   1 bar (3 ounces) coffee-flavored chocolate, finely chopped

Glaze

   1 teaspoon freeze-dried or instant coffee granules

   1 to 2 tablespoons half-and-half

   ⅛ teaspoon salt

   ½ cup powdered sugar

1. Preheat oven to 350°F. Lightly grease cookie sheets.

2. For cookies, beat butter and sugars in large bowl with electric mixer at medium speed until creamy. Add egg and vanilla; beat until blended, scraping down side of bowl once. Combine flour, salt and baking soda in bowl. Gradually add flour mixture to butter mixture, beating until blended. Stir in pecans and chocolate.

3. Drop dough by tablespoons 3 inches apart onto prepared cookie sheets. Bake 10 to 12 minutes or until set and lightly browned. Cool 5 minutes on cookie sheets. Remove to wire racks to cool completely.

4. For glaze, mix coffee, 1 tablespoon half-and-half and salt in microwavable bowl. Microwave at HIGH 15 seconds or until coffee dissolves. Stir in powdered sugar until smooth. If necessary, stir in remaining half-and-half by teaspoons until desired glaze consistency is reached. Drizzle glaze over cookies. Let stand 30 minutes or until set. *Makes 3 dozen cookies*

Mocha Madness

Butterscotch Almond Crescents

Cookies
   1 cup (2 sticks) unsalted butter, softened
   ½ cup plus 1 tablespoon powdered sugar
   ¼ teaspoon salt
   1 teaspoon almond extract
   1¾ cups all-purpose flour
   ¾ cup ground almonds

Glaze
   ½ cup packed light brown sugar
   2 tablespoons half-and-half
   1½ tablespoons unsalted butter
   ¼ teaspoon salt
   ½ cup sliced almonds

1. Preheat oven to 300°F. Line cookie sheets with parchment paper.

2. For cookies, beat butter, powdered sugar and salt in large bowl with electric mixer at medium speed until light and fluffy. Add almond extract; beat until blended. Gradually add flour, beating until well blended. Stir in ground almonds until well blended.

3. Shape tablespoonfuls dough into 3-inch ropes. Shape ropes into crescents; place on prepared cookie sheets. Bake 20 to 25 minutes or until lightly browned. Cool 5 minutes on cookie sheets; transfer to wire racks to cool completely.

4. For glaze, combine brown sugar, half-and-half, butter and salt in small saucepan. Cook over low heat, stirring constantly, until butter melts and sugar dissolves.

5. Drizzle glaze over crescents; sprinkle with almonds. Let stand 30 minutes or until glaze is set.   *Makes 3 to 3½ dozen cookies*

Chocolate Gingerbread Cookies

½ cup (1 stick) unsalted butter, softened
½ cup packed light brown sugar
¼ cup granulated sugar
1 tablespoon shortening
4 ounces semisweet chocolate, melted and cooled
2 tablespoons molasses
1 egg
2¼ cups all-purpose flour
3 tablespoons unsweetened cocoa powder
2½ teaspoons ground ginger
½ teaspoon baking soda
½ teaspoon ground cinnamon
⅛ teaspoon salt
⅛ teaspoon finely ground pepper
  Prepared icing (optional)

1. Beat butter, sugars and shortening in large bowl with electric mixer at medium speed until creamy. Add chocolate; beat until blended. Add molasses and egg; beat until well blended. Combine flour, cocoa, ginger, baking soda, cinnamon, salt and pepper in medium bowl. Gradually add flour mixture to butter mixture, beating until well blended. Divide dough in half. Wrap each half in plastic wrap; refrigerate at least 1 hour.

2. Preheat oven to 350°F. Roll out one dough half between plastic wrap until about ¼ inch thick. Cut dough with 5-inch cookie cutters; place cutouts on ungreased cookie sheets. Refrigerate at least 15 minutes. Repeat with remaining dough.

3. Bake 8 to 10 minutes or until cookies have puffed slightly and have small cracks on surfaces. Cool 5 minutes on cookie sheets. Remove to wire racks to cool completely. Decorate cooled cookies with icing, if desired.   *Makes about 2 dozen 5-inch cookies*

Chocolate Gingerbread Cookies

Candy-Studded Wreaths

1 cup (2 sticks) unsalted butter, softened
½ cup powdered sugar
2 tablespoons packed light brown sugar
¼ teaspoon salt
1 teaspoon vanilla
2 cups all-purpose flour
4 to 5 drops green food coloring
    Mini candy-coated chocolate pieces

1. Beat butter, powdered sugar, brown sugar and salt in large bowl with electric mixer at medium speed until light and fluffy. Add vanilla; beat until well blended. Add flour, ½ cup at a time, beating well after each addition.

2. Divide dough in half. Tint half of dough with food coloring to desired shade of green. Leave remaining half of dough plain. If dough is too soft, wrap in plastic wrap and refrigerate about 1 hour.

3. Preheat oven to 300°F. Shape green dough into 28 (5-inch) ropes. Repeat with plain dough. For each wreath, twist one green and one plain rope together; press ends together. Place on ungreased cookie sheet. Press 4 to 6 chocolate pieces into each wreath. Bake 15 to 18 minutes or until lightly browned. Cool 5 minutes on cookie sheets. Remove to wire racks to cool completely.   *Makes 28 cookies*

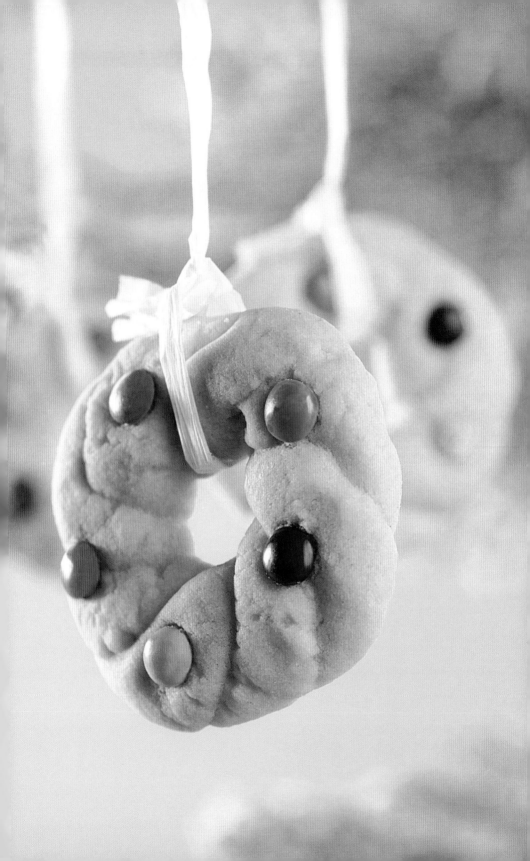

Dark Chocolate Dreams

16 ounces bittersweet chocolate candy bars, coarsely
chopped or bittersweet chocolate chips
¼ cup (½ stick) butter
½ cup all-purpose flour
¾ teaspoon ground cinnamon
½ teaspoon baking powder
¼ teaspoon salt
1½ cups sugar
3 eggs
1 teaspoon vanilla
1 package (12 ounces) white chocolate chips
1 cup chopped pecans, lightly toasted

1. Preheat oven to 350°F. Grease cookie sheets or line with
parchment paper.

2. Place chocolate and butter in large microwavable bowl.
Microwave at HIGH 2 minutes; stir. Microwave 1 to 2 minutes,
stirring after 1 minute, or until chocolate is melted. Let cool slightly.

3. Combine flour, cinnamon, baking powder and salt in small
bowl; set aside.

4. Beat sugar, eggs and vanilla with electric mixer at medium-high
speed about 6 minutes or until very thick and mixture turns pale
color. Reduce speed to low; slowly beat in chocolate mixture until
well blended. Gradually beat in flour mixture until blended. Fold in
white chocolate chips and pecans.

5. Drop dough, 3 inches apart, by level ⅓ cupfuls onto prepared
cookie sheets. Place piece of plastic wrap over dough; flatten
dough with fingertips to form 4-inch circles. Remove plastic wrap.

6. Bake 12 minutes or until just firm to the touch and surface begins
to crack. *Do not overbake.* Cool 2 minutes on cookie sheets. Remove
to wire racks; cool completely. *Makes 10 to 12 (5-inch) cookies*